This book belongs to:

_____

First Edition Published by KDP - 2021

Copyright © Karen Benedict - 2021

All rights reserved, this book or parts thereof may not be reproduced or used in any manner without written permission from the publisher.

First paperback edition October 2021

ISBN 978-1-7777605-8-8 Hardcover
ISBN 978-1-7777605-7-1 Paperback
ISBN 978-1-7777605-6-4 EBook

Thank you for buying an authorized edition of this book and for complying with copyright laws by not reproducing, scanning or distributing any part of it in any form without permission. You are supporting writers by doing this.

Published by Birdhouse Press

I dedicate this book to
Mom and Dad:

Christmas time brings back cherished memories of being raised in a small town. I could hardly wait to start decorating the Christmas tree every year.
Thank you for the lovely memories!

"Wow, these ornaments sure are old! William said, opening a dusty box. As he brushed off the box, Katie let out a big sneeze!

"God bless you," Mom said. "I hope you're not getting sick!" Katie shook her head. "No, it's just the dust."

Her nose still twitching, Katie reached for the box. "I'm so excited. My friend, Tasha, showed me a picture of her tree. It has a ton of beautiful glittery ornaments. It's so pretty. I hope our tree looks just like hers!"

But when Katie unwrapped her first ornament, she began to frown. "Why did you want to keep this one?" she asked as a clunky piece of dried clay fell onto her lap.

"It's so ugly! And look, someone scribbled all over it!"

"I love that ornament!" Katie's mom said. "You made it when you were just three years old. The scribbling is yours!"

Mom took the ornament from Katie and hung it on the tree with pride.

Katie made a face
at her handmade ornament
reached into the box
for another one.
There's got to be something better
in here somewhere!"

Katie unwrapped ornament after ornament, each more disappointing than the last. There was not a single shimmery, dazzling one in the box.

"Do we have to hang these up on the tree?" Katie asked.

"They're all so junky!"

"Why can't we have ornaments like the ones at the store?"

"hmmmm..."

"Because Christmas isn't about looking pretty, or looking like everyone else," Mom said.

"It's our special tradition to hang up these ornaments," Katie's Dad added.

"Each one is unique. And they bring back so many good memories. Not like the ones you can buy at the store. Those are so cold. They have no meaning."

Katie crossed her arms.
"Well, maybe we should make a tradition of getting new ones," she said, sulking...
"Looking nice means something to me."

Just then, William pulled another ornament out of the box.

"Hey, look at this one!" he said, "My teacher, Ms. Johnson gave this to me last year. She was my favorite teacher."

William happily stood and hung the ornament on the tree.

"Here's another special one," Mom said.
"Remember when Ollie tried to eat the Christmas cookies one year?" she asked, laughing.
"This was the only one we saved from getting eaten!"

"Oh, yeah!" Katie said, laughing in spite of herself. "Those cookies smelled so good. I really wanted to eat one!"

Katie watched William dig around in the ornament box.
"Uh-oh," he said.
"It looks like this one is broken."
Dad took it carefully in his hands.

"It might look broken,
but it's actually a very special ornament.
It was given to me by my great-grandmother.
Check this out."

He tilted the jar
to show Katie and William the
old melted candle hiding inside.
"What's so exciting about
an old candle in a jar?"
Katie asked.

"Well, it happens to be the most important ornament we have in this house," Dad said. "Because it reminds us of the true meaning of Christmas."

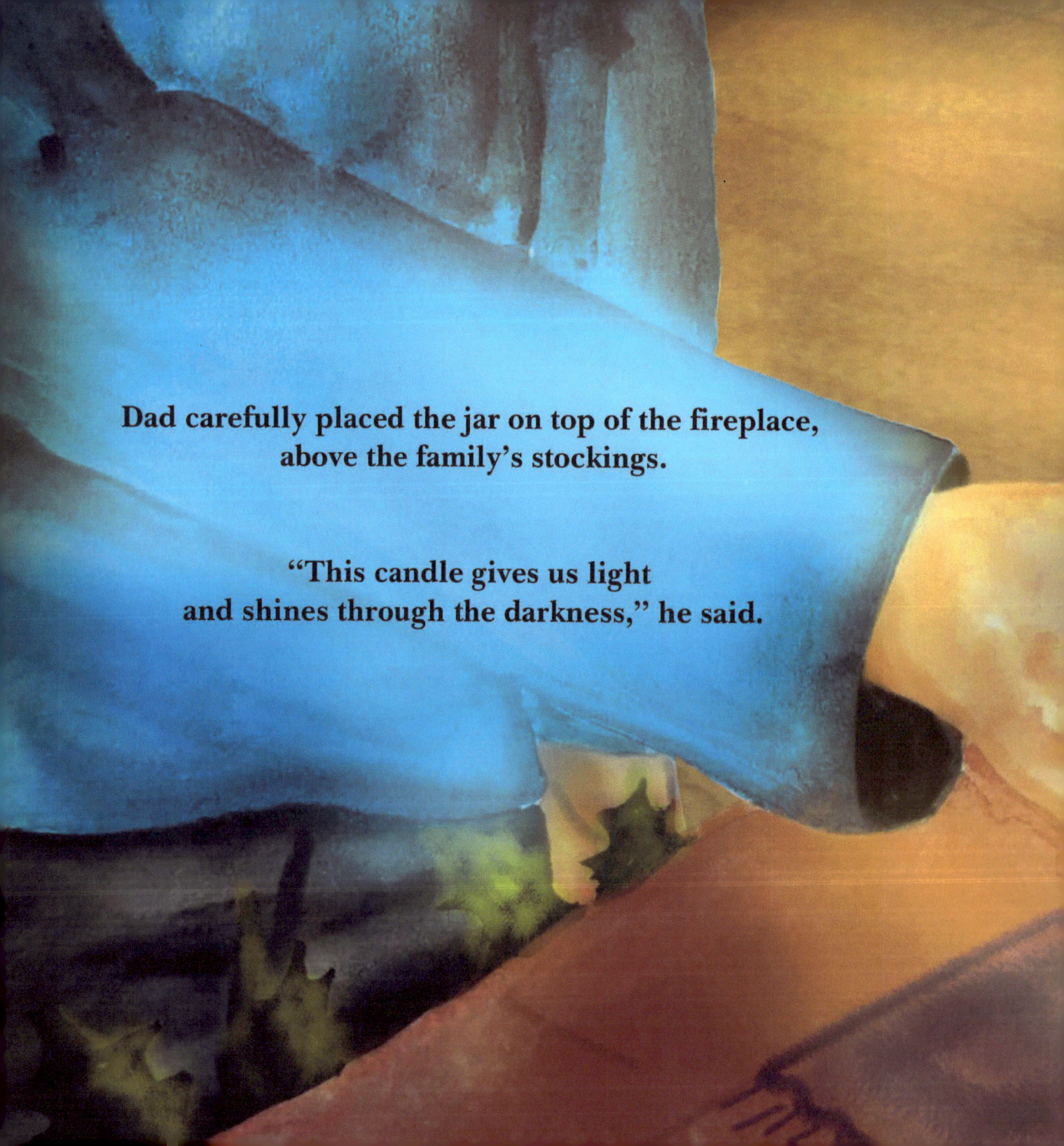

Dad carefully placed the jar on top of the fireplace, above the family's stockings.

"This candle gives us light and shines through the darkness," he said.

"Every Christmas,
we take time
to remember another light
that came into the world
when our savior,
Jesus, was born."

Katie and William watched as he lit the candle.
"Jesus said in the Bible,
'I am the light of the world.
He who follows me will not walk in darkness,
but will have the light of life.'"

Katie watched the flickering light in the old jar.
She had to admit,
it was beautiful, in its own way.
It made her wonder . . .
had she forgotten
what Christmas was really about?

Katie and William each took a candle from the carolers' basket.

Together, they sang "Silent Night," over the warm glow of the candles.

Above them, soft snow began to fall.
For Katie, it was a beautiful sight, almost magical.
At that moment she knew what she had been missing.

Before the carolers left,
they handed Katie a tiny angel ornament.
It didn't seem like much,
but Katie was thrilled to have it.

"I have an idea," she said,
smiling up at her mom.
Walking over to the tree,
she placed the angel
right next to her childhood
ornament.

"Everybody ready?" Dad asked.

He turned on the Christmas lights, and the tree began to sparkle!

Katie sat back on the couch to look at the tree.
One by one, the rest of the family,
including Ollie, joined her.

"Wow," Katie exclaimed.
"You can see all of our ornaments so nicely from here."
"You don't think they look tacky?" her mom asked.

"Not at all," Katie said. "They really do bring back good memories. You're right. That's better than any of the sparkly ornaments you'd get from the store. I hope when we hang up our angel ornament next year, we'll remember how good this day was, too."

www.ingramcontent.com/pod-product-compliance
Lightning Source LLC
Chambersburg PA
CBHW041704160426

43209CB00017B/1746